GREAT
AMERICAN PRESIDENTS

JOHN
ADAMS

GREAT
AMERICAN PRESIDENTS

JOHN ADAMS

JOHN QUINCY ADAMS

JIMMY CARTER

THOMAS JEFFERSON

JOHN F. KENNEDY

ABRAHAM LINCOLN

RONALD REAGAN

FRANKLIN DELANO ROOSEVELT

THEODORE ROOSEVELT

HARRY S. TRUMAN

GEORGE WASHINGTON

WOODROW WILSON

GREAT
AMERICAN PRESIDENTS

JOHN
ADAMS

HEATHER LEHR WAGNER

FOREWORD BY
WALTER CRONKITE

CHELSEA HOUSE
P U B L I S H E R S
A Haights Cross Communications Company

Philadelphia

CHELSEA HOUSE PUBLISHERS

VP, NEW PRODUCT DEVELOPMENT Sally Cheney
DIRECTOR OF PRODUCTION Kim Shinners
CREATIVE MANAGER Takeshi Takahashi
MANUFACTURING MANAGER Diann Grasse

STAFF FOR JOHN ADAMS

ASSOCIATE EDITOR Kate Sullivan
PRODUCTION ASSISTANT Megan Emery
PHOTO EDITOR Sarah Bloom
SERIES DESIGNER Keith Trego
COVER DESIGNER Keith Trego
LAYOUT 21st Century Publishing and Communications, Inc.

A Haights Cross Communications ⌁ Company

www.chelseahouse.com

First Printing

1 3 5 7 9 8 6 4 2

Library of Congress Cataloging-in-Publication Data

Wagner, Heather Lehr.
    John Adams/by Heather Lehr Wagner.
       p. cm.—(Great American presidents)
Includes bibliographical references and index.
    ISBN 0-7910-7603-2 — ISBN 0-7910-7787-X (pbk.)
    1. Adams, John, 1735-1826—Juvenile literature. 2. Presidents—United States—
Biography—Juvenile literature. [1. Adams, John, 1735–1826. 2. Presidents.] I. Title. II. Series.
E322.W23 2003
973.4'4'092—dc21
                                                                         2003014157

TABLE OF CONTENTS

FOREWORD

WALTER CRONKITE

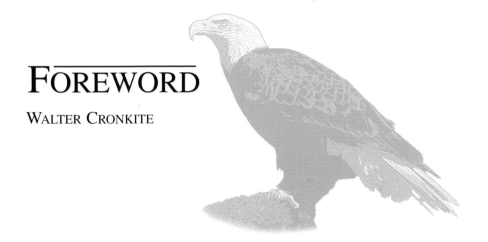

A candle can defy the darkness. It need not have the power of a great searchlight to be a welcome break from the gloom of night. So it goes in the assessment of leadership. He who lights the candle may not have the skill or imagination to turn the light that flickers for a moment into a perpetual glow, but history will assign credit to the degree it is due.

Some of our great American presidents may have had a single moment that bridged the chasm between the ordinary and the exceptional. Others may have assured their lofty place in our history through the sum total of their accomplishments.

When asked who were our greatest presidents, we cannot fail to open our list with the Founding Fathers who put together this nation and nursed it through the difficult years of its infancy. George Washington, John Adams, Thomas Jefferson, and James Madison took the high principles of the revolution against British tyranny and turned the concept of democracy into a nation that became the beacon of hope to oppressed peoples around the globe.

Almost invariably we add to that list our wartime presidents — Abraham Lincoln, perhaps Woodrow Wilson, and certainly Franklin Delano Roosevelt.

Nonetheless there is a thread of irony that runs through the inclusion of the names of those wartime presidents: In many aspects their leadership was enhanced by the fact that, without objection from the people, they assumed extraordinary powers to pursue victory over the nation's enemies (or, in the case of Lincoln, the Southern states).

The complexities of the democratic procedures by which the United States Constitution deliberately tried to withhold unchecked power from the presidency encumbered the presidents who needed their hands freed of the entangling bureaucracy that is the federal government.

Much of our history is written far after the events themselves took place. History may be amended by a much later generation seeking a precedent to justify an action considered necessary at the latter time. The history, in a sense, becomes what later generations interpret it to be.

President Jefferson in 1803 negotiated the purchase of vast lands in the south and west of North America from the French. The deal became knows as the Louisiana Purchase. A century and a half later, to justify seizing the nation's steel mills that were being shut down by a labor strike, President Truman cited the Louisiana Purchase as a case when the president in a major matter ignored Congress and acted almost solely on his own authority.

The case went to the Supreme Court, which overturned Truman six to three. The chief justice, Fred Vinson, was one of the three justices who supported the president. Many historians, however, agreed with the court's majority, pointing out that Jefferson scarcely acted alone: Members of Congress were in the forefront of the agitation to consummate the Louisiana Purchase and Congress voted to fund it.

With more than two centuries of history and precedent now behind us, the Constitution is still found to be flexible when honest and sincere individuals support their own causes with quite different readings of it. These are the questions that end up for interpretation by the Supreme Court.

As late as the early years of the twenty-first century, perhaps the most fateful decision any president ever can make—to commit the nation to war—was again debated and precedent ignored. The Constitution says that only the Congress has the authority to declare war. Yet the Congress, with the objection of few members, ignored this Constitutional provision and voted to give President George W. Bush the right to take the United States to war whenever and under whatever conditions he decided.

Thus a president's place in history may well be determined by how much power he seizes or is granted in re-interpreting and circumventing the remarkable document that is the Constitution. Although the Founding Fathers thought they had spelled out the president's authority in their clear division of powers between the branches of the executive, the legislative and the judiciary, their wisdom has been challenged frequently by ensuing generations. The need and the demand for change is dictated by the march of events, the vast alterations in society, the global condition beyond our influence, and the progress of technology far beyond the imaginations of any of the generations which preceded them.

The extent to which the powers of the presidency will be enhanced and utilized by the chief executives to come in large degree will depend, as they have throughout our history, on the character of the presidents themselves. The limitations on those powers, in turn, will depend on the strength and will of those other two legs of the three-legged stool of American government — the legislative and the judiciary.

And as long as this nation remains a democracy, the final say will rest with an educated electorate in perpetual exercise of its constitutional rights to free speech and a free and alert press.

1

A WISE AND
HONEST MAN

IT WAS EARLY in the afternoon of November 1, 1800, when a coach pulled by four horses drove up to the large house set in a weedy field. Inside the coach were two men, and another man followed them on horseback. There were no welcoming crowds to greet them, nor was there any kind of ceremony to mark this important occasion. John Adams, the first president to occupy the building that would one day be known as the White House, had arrived in Washington, D.C.

Workmen were still busy plastering and painting what was then called the "President's House," and while it was an imposing structure, it was still incomplete. The field surrounding the house

John Adams was the second president of the United States and the first president to live in the White House, at that time called the President's House. It was still under construction when Adams became president in 1797. He moved into the President's House, which developed from many of George Washington's ideas, in late 1800.

was dotted with stones and marked with wagon ruts. The rooms inside smelled strongly of wet paint, and many of the closets were missing doors. The furniture Adams had sent on from his Philadelphia residence seemed small and out of place in the massive rooms. Upstairs and downstairs were connected by one small staircase at the back of the house. And the only decoration on the walls was a huge portrait of Adams' predecessor, the man to whom he had often been unfavorably compared: George Washington.

In fact, the President's House had been Washington's creation, although he never occupied it. It was Washington who had decided (over the objections of many) that the building would be made of whitewashed stone. There were not many homes or buildings constructed from smooth stone in the late eighteenth century. Homes were built from wood or, less often, brick. Stone construction in public buildings would not become popular until nearly a century later. But Washington had wanted the President's House to stand out. He approved the elaborate stone ornaments and carvings, the designs of oak leaves and flowers, and the fancy "hoods" over the windows to ensure that the home of the president of the new United States was the most noteworthy and finest to be found anywhere in the country.

It was an impressive residence, but on the night President John Adams arrived, it proved a bit lacking in ceremony. Adams met with two members of his cabinet and then, after an informal supper, he took a candle and climbed the back stairs to his bedroom.

Building and leading a new nation was difficult and sometimes lonely. Adams' beloved wife, Abigail, had not yet joined him in Washington, D.C., and he missed her company. When they were apart, their letters back and forth kept them connected and frequently proved vital to Adams during difficult times. And so, the very next morning, the president sat at his desk in his new office and wrote to her. The letter contained a description of his journey to Washington and expressed his belief that the President's House, although not finished, would be acceptable. He told Abigail that he hoped she would be able to join him as soon as possible. Adams ended his letter with a phrase that would eventually be carved on the mantelpiece of the

White House, a prayer for the future leaders that would call this new building their home: *"I pray to heaven to bestow the best of blessings on this house and all that shall hereafter inhabit it. May none but honest and wise men ever rule under this roof."*

SMALL-TOWN LIFE

The man who would write this blessing for the President's House was born in the small village of Braintree, Massachusetts, on October 19, 1735. The Adams family had an established history in Braintree. They were one of the earliest Puritan families to settle in the region. The young John Adams' great-great-grandfather, Henry Adams, had arrived in Braintree in 1638 with his wife and nine children, seeking to build a community of faith in the new Massachusetts Bay Colony. Only his youngest son, Joseph, remained in Braintree, but he would father a line of dedicated men who worked as farmers.

The future president's father, also named John Adams, was the deacon of the Congregational Church and played an important role in Braintree's community. In addition to farming his 50 acres of land, Deacon John had served as a tax collector and militia officer, and was elected nine times to Braintree's board of selectmen (a local governing body).

By the time young John was born, the village of Braintree had grown to about 2,000 people. The Adams home was quite similar to the others in the village. Built in 1681, it was a five-room saltbox-style house. On the ground floor were three rooms with two large fireplaces;

13

John Adams was born on October 19, 1735, on this farm in Braintree, Massachusetts, outside of Boston. His great-great-grandfather arrived in Braintree in 1638 with his wife and nine children. John inherited the house upon his father's death in 1761.

upstairs were two rooms shared by John and his younger brothers—Peter, born in 1738, and Elihu, born in 1744. The bedrooms were stifling hot in the summer and freezing in the winter.

His parents taught John the value of hard work, and his mother taught him to read when he was five years old. John spent much of his early childhood outdoors, flying kites, skating on frozen ponds, hunting, fishing, and swimming. John was bright and quick to learn, and his father soon decided that John should be better educated than he himself had been. He wanted his son to go to college.

When John was about six years old, he went to a "dame school." This was a kind of primary school for boys and girls, held at a teacher's house. Lessons were based on *The New England Primer,* a book that combined principles of reading and writing with Puritan religious beliefs. Children spent hours memorizing and reciting phrases like "He who ne'er learns his ABCs, forever will a blockhead be."

Soon young John graduated from the dame school and was enrolled in the Braintree Latin School, one of two types of schools available to young students in those days. Students in the Latin schools (as opposed to the more common "public schools") were prepared for college. Most would become clergymen or lawyers, and so they spent six to eight years studying Latin and Greek.

John did not like his teacher or his school and spent the school days dreaming. He wanted to leave school and one day told his father that he had decided to become a farmer.

The following day, John's father invited him to help him on the farm. The two spent the hot day working in the marsh, struggling through knee-deep mud to cut, lift and tie the bundles of thatch. At the end of that long, exhausting day, John's father asked him how he liked farming. When John responded that he liked it very well, his father replied, "Ay, but I don't like it so well. You shall go to school."

When his father later realized that it was the teacher, not the school, that John disliked, he enrolled him in a different school where John's work rapidly improved, so much so that within 18 months, at the age of 15, he was ready to apply to college. This meant Harvard—the only college in the region.

John was no more excited at the prospect of college than he had been about any other part of his schooling, but, knowing that his father would be terribly disappointed if he gave up on his education, he rode on horseback to Cambridge to apply to Harvard in person. The application process consisted of an interview with the college president and a few professors—a frightening experience that John passed. He rode home with the happy news that he had been accepted.

The class John joined at Harvard consisted of 27 young men who, like him, were about 14 or 15 years old. It was an elite group—few young men went to college in those days. John did well at Harvard. He found a new love for books and studying, especially enjoying mathematics and science. He made friends and was disappointed when the four years came to an end. He was also uncertain—he had not decided on a career. His father had assumed that John would become a clergyman, but a career in the church did not appeal to John. Some of John's friends and professors had suggested that he study law. John liked the idea of a career that promised some financial rewards and public recognition, and he knew that he had a talent for public speaking.

But in order to study law, John had to pay a fee to be taken into the office of a practicing attorney. John needed to earn the money, so he took a job as a teacher in Worcester, Massachusetts, in the summer of 1755. It was a dramatic change from the lively, academic environment of Cambridge. Furthermore, John had little talent for teaching, and he found himself struggling to stay motivated.

Finally, in the summer of 1756, shortly before his 21st birthday, John signed a two-year contract with a young Worcester attorney named James Putnam. He moved in with Putnam, studying with him at night and continuing to teach during the day. When the two years had passed, John returned to Braintree. He was admitted to the bar on November 6, 1759, and this allowed him to practice law.

> *"All that part of creation which lies within our observation, is liable to change. Even mighty states and kingdoms are not exempted.*
>
> *If we look into history, we shall find some nations rising from contemptible beginnings, and spreading their influence till the whole globe is subjected to their sway. When they have reached the summit of grandeur, some minute and unsuspected cause commonly effects their ruin, and the empire of the world is transferred to some other place."*
>
> — While John Adams worked as a teacher in Worchester, he became increasingly interested in politics, as reflected in this letter written to a friend on October 12, 1755.

A WORKING LAWYER

John's first months as a lawyer were anxious ones. He had few clients, and he struggled to make his business grow. John's first case did not go well. When the court ruled against his client, John was devastated.

Even greater devastation came on May 25, 1761, when John's father died of influenza. The illness had swept through Braintree in an epidemic, killing 16 other people in town in addition to Deacon John and leaving John's mother so ill and weak that she could not attend the funeral.

His father's death meant that John was now the head of the family. He was also a property owner—his father's will had left John the house next door to the family farm and 40 acres of land. As a property owner, John could participate in town meetings and he was soon appointed to serve as Braintree's surveyor of highways. John set up his law practice in the former kitchen of his home. John's practice soon grew and he traveled to Boston once or twice a week, studying cases and carrying out legal business.

He also kept busy traveling on horseback five miles to and from Weymouth to visit a young woman named Abigail Smith. John had first met Abigail in 1759, when she was 15 years old. At the time, John had been much more interested in Abigail's second cousin, Hannah Quincy. But two years later, Abigail and John were reintroduced by a friend of John's, who was courting Abigail's older sister. Abigail, now a more mature 17-year-old, was an avid reader, who loved to talk and was every bit as stubborn as the 27-year-old lawyer.

John and Abigail soon fell in love and exchanged frequent letters full of admiration. Abigail was intelligent and cheerful; she admired John and believed that the short, stout lawyer would achieve great things. They decided to marry.

On October 25, 1764, John and Abigail Adams married. They immediately moved to John's home in Braintree, and while John focused on the farm and his law practice, Abigail spent her days as most New England women of that time did—rising at five, sewing, baking, feeding the chickens, and churning butter. On July 14, 1765, their first child, a daughter they named Abigail (nicknamed Nabby), was born.

But the year would bring even greater change. In May of 1765, the American colonists learned that England had

John Adams first met Abigail Smith in 1759, when she was 15 years old. They met again two years later, fell in love, and were married on October 25, 1764. Their first child, Abigail, whom they called Nabby, was born on July 14, 1765.

passed a new tax called the Stamp Act. This tax would mark the beginning of what would become a revolution; it would also mark a new chapter in the life of John Adams.

2

A PATRIOT'S CHALLENGE

FROM 1756 TO 1763, English troops had fought French forces in America (where the French were joined by Indian tribes), as well as in Russia, Spain, Portugal, Austria, Prussia and much of Germany. This lengthy war was known as the French and Indian War in the American colonies and the Seven Years' War in Europe. When the conflict finally ended, England was faced with a crushing debt, the cost of fighting on so many fronts for so many years.

Because the conflict had "officially" begun in America (in an attack led by a young colonial soldier named George Washington), many in England believed that the colonists should have the

The British government passed the Stamp Act in November 1765, causing widespread riots in the colonies. The Stamp Act, imposed to pay for the Seven Years' War, required that certain products—most those made of paper—carried an official stamp, which increased the cost of those products.

responsibility of repaying some of the war debt. The English Parliament agreed, and the Stamp Act, instituting the new tax, was passed.

The tax went into effect in November 1765, and it affected nearly every colonist. Almost every official document and piece of business printed on paper—newspapers, advertisements, bills, legal documents, deeds, diplomas, even playing cards—had to carry an official stamp. The stamp was expensive and increased the cost of printing and distributing most documents and other paper products.

Riots swept through the colonies in protest of the tax. While many reacted with violence, 30-year-old John Adams responded with reason and careful thought, outlining his ideas in an essay entitled *A Dissertation on the Canon and the Feudal Law*. The Stamp Act, although certainly the inspiration for some of Adams' thoughts, was not the focus of his essay. Instead, Adams discussed what he believed was the basis for certain American freedoms and rights—British law—and that the liberty all Americans should enjoy was God-given and had been earned by the sacrifice of generations of Americans.

Adams' essay was published in the *Boston Gazette* on August 12, 1765, and soon brought great attention to its author. Adams found himself part of a new circle of political activists based in Boston, a group that included his second cousin, Samuel Adams.

Because of widespread opposition, the British Parliament was finally forced to repeal the Stamp Act in early 1766. John Adams was able to turn his attention

> *"No one of any feeling, born and educated in this once happy country, can consider the numerous distresses, the gross indignities, the barbarous ignorance, the haughty usurpations, that we have reason to fear are meditating for ourselves, our children, our neighbors, in short, for all our countrymen and all their posterity, without the utmost agonies of heart and many tears."*
>
> — John Adams' essay, *Dissertation on the Canon and the Feudal Law*, published in the August 1765 *Boston Gazette*. In it, Adams agrees that British law guarantees certain basic rights.

back to his law practice. In 1768, the family moved to Boston. That same year, British troops arrived in Boston, sent to ensure that no more protests greeted yet another British tax to be placed on paper, tea, paint and glass. The visible presence of red-coated troops marching through Boston left a clear impression in the colony of Massachusetts that King George III held little love for his colonial subjects and would rule them by force.

Trouble erupted on the evening of March 5, 1770. A small crowd of men and boys gathered outside the Boston Customs House, heckling the one British guard on duty. A fire alarm bell began to sound, and more men and boys quickly appeared, carrying clubs and sticks. Soon, a crowd of several hundred had gathered. The guard was joined by eight other British soldiers and a captain, all armed with loaded muskets and bayonets.

The crowd cursed the soldiers and threw snowballs and stones at them. Then someone threw a club, which hit one of the soldiers. Suddenly shots rang out. Several people in the crowd were hit by musket balls and five men were killed. The British commander, Thomas Preston, quickly yelled at his men to cease their fire, and then marched them away. The wounded were carried off, and the stunned crowd, after milling around for a few hours, finally dispersed.

The next day, as violence simmered in the air, John Adams was asked if he would serve as the defense lawyer for the soldiers and their captain when their trial was held. No other lawyer had been willing to take the case. Adams accepted, believing that the case would be important and that it would prove a test of the right of all men to legal representation and a fair trial.

Ultimately, two trials were held—the first for the British commander, Thomas Preston, who had been accused of giving the order to fire, and the second for the soldiers. Adams' decision to serve as the defense attorney in both cases was quite risky, both professionally and personally. His plea for Captain Preston resulted in a "not guilty" verdict. Adams' closing arguments in defense of the soldiers were even more impressive. He argued that the mob must bear some responsibility for what had happened. But Adams also noted that the mob had gathered because of the British government's policy of sending in soldiers to keep the peace.

Six of the soldiers were found not guilty. Two were charged with manslaughter. Adams was pleased with the results, and his legal practice and reputation in Boston quickly grew. Soon he was representing some of the wealthiest men in the colony. In the summer of 1770, Adams was elected to the Massachusetts state legislature.

A POLITICAL LIFE

Adams struggled to balance the demands of his legal practice and his political role in Boston. His family was growing, too. His first son, John Quincy, was born in 1767; his second daughter, Susanna, was born in 1768.

Two more sons, Charles and Thomas, joined the family in 1770 and 1772.

While Adams wanted to focus on his business and family rather than on politics, political events in Boston made this increasingly difficult. A tax on tea resulted in the famous dumping of tea into Boston Harbor in December 1773. By May 1774, England had closed Boston Harbor, creating a blockade of ships around the city. That same year, the Massachusetts legislature elected a group of five delegates to attend a meeting in Philadelphia, where representatives from all the colonies gathered to discuss how best to respond to British oppression. John Adams was one of the delegates chosen to attend the First Continental Congress. Adams made the 15-day journey to Philadelphia, not realizing that he was setting out on a path that would change his nation's destiny—and his own—forever.

The 55 delegates to the First Continental Congress were mostly moderate men, concerned by England's recent actions but generally still loyal to the king. While they agreed with Adams that Americans possessed certain basic rights, they were quite divided as to how best express their concerns to England. Adams and the others from Massachusetts were regarded as the most radical of the delegates, since the most violent protests—and the strongest crackdowns from the British military—had been centered in their colony.

The meetings began on September 5, and quickly settled into a slow routine of seemingly endless

Patrick Henry is shown speaking here at the First Constitutional Convention, held in Philadelphia in 1774. Adams and the other delegates from Massachusetts, who advocated the rights of the colonies, were considered radicals at the convention, where most of the men were hesitant to be disloyal to England.

speeches. Adams grew impatient with the debates required over even the smallest issues. With so many great speechmakers gathered in one place, every discussion broke down into an opportunity for the delegates to demonstrate their verbal skills. Every day ended with a great dinner, and the constant feasting and social activities also began to wear on Adams. He was relieved when the convention recessed in late October and he could go home.

While Adams was in Massachusetts, conflict again broke out between the colonial militia and the British army. When the British learned that the militia was storing gunpowder and weapons in the town of Concord, British soldiers set out from Boston to capture the arms. An alarm alerting the colonists about the pending attack was sounded by Paul Revere and William Dawes, and by the time the soldiers arrived at the town of Lexington, the militia (known as minutemen) had assembled. Eight Americans were killed in the gunfire that followed before the British soldiers marched on to Concord. There, local farmers and militia began firing on them, forcing them back to Boston. The "shot heard round the world" had been fired; the colony of Massachusetts seemed committed to a revolution.

In May 1775, Adams returned to Philadelphia for the Second Continental Congress. The mood among the delegates was quite different now, deeply affected by the events in Massachusetts. But the delegates were not yet unified. Some still believed in the possibility of negotiating with the king and Parliament, while others were determined to separate from England.

Adams grew increasingly impatient with his fellow delegates as news from Abigail told of a colony under attack. The Massachusetts militia was in desperate need of supplies and arms. Adams wanted Congress to make the militia its own to ensure that it represented not just one but all of the colonies.

Adams decided that the best way to ensure that the

delegates were unified and understood that the conflict was not simply a Massachusetts problem was to nominate a military commander for the new army, someone from a colony other than Massachusetts. Virginia was the logical choice—it was the largest colony, it would represent the southern colonies, and many of its delegates had demonstrated their support for the Massachusetts militia's actions.

Thus, on June 14, 1775, John Adams stood up to nominate George Washington of Virginia to serve as commander in chief of the Continental Army. The motion was quickly seconded. Washington had impressed Adams with his willingness to risk his fortune in the conflict; he had demonstrated his leadership skills during the French and Indian War, and Adams appreciated Washington's quiet care in discussing the problems between America and England. Adams felt certain that Washington would appreciate the enormity of the task facing him and be worthy of the new post. Washington traveled to Massachusetts on July 2 and took command of the new Continental Army the next day.

The next months flew by as Adams was absorbed in meetings, serving as chairman of some 25 committees while participating as a member of several others. The pace of work was overwhelming, and Adams was frequently sick. He traveled home twice when Congress adjourned, returning to Philadelphia in early February 1776.

Upon his return, Adams drew up a "to do" list, detailing in his diary the things he believed needed to be accomplished. Among these were forming an alliance with France and Spain, building gunpowder mills in every colony, and drafting a "Declaration of Independency."

3

FIGHTING FOR FREEDOM

JOHN ADAMS WAS not the only delegate who was considering independence in that early part of 1776. In January of that year, Thomas Paine had published the pamphlet *Common Sense*, which spelled out the arguments for independence in plain language. Adams felt Paine's arguments were a bit too simplistic. Adams drafted his own pamphlet, titled *Thoughts on Government*, a document that described the new system of government he thought would best serve the colonies—a government with two branches designed to provide checks and balances to each other.

As sickness (including smallpox) spread through Philadelphia— and through the Congress—word came to the delegates that the royal governor of Virginia had promised all slaves their freedom if they joined the British forces. He had also ordered an attack on the city of Norfolk, Virginia. Further bad news followed. The British Parliament had outlawed all trade with the colonies and declared that any colonist who did not immediately declare his loyalty to the king was a traitor and faced hanging.

Other rumors soon followed. It was widely believed that England was sending a fleet of ships across the Atlantic and that a treaty had been made that would bring German soldiers to help support the British army's efforts in America. To Adams, the need for a declaration of independence seemed clear, but he wisely understood that many viewed the Massachusetts delegation as a group of radicals. This meant that he must control his temper and outspokenness and allow others to take the lead. The Congress still seemed deeply divided, and radical opinions from a radical Massachusetts delegation would not unite it.

Then, on June 7, the Virginia delegate Richard Henry Lee rose and offered the motion that the colonies "are, and

> *"We ought to consider what is the end of government, before we determine which is the best form. Upon this point all speculative politicians will agree that the happiness of society is the end of government. . . . From this principle it will follow that the form of government which communicates ease, comfort, security, or, in one word, happiness, to the greatest number of persons, and in the greatest degree, is the best."*
>
> — In 1776, John Adams outlined his plan for a new, republican form of government as a response to Thomas Paine's pamphlet *Common Sense.* Adams' *Thoughts on Government* detailed how the colonial government might be shaped into something new.

of a right ought to be, free and independent states . . . and that all political connection between them and the state of Great Britain is, and ought to be, totally dissolved." Intense debate followed. It was finally decided that while the delegates awaited instructions from their home colonies about whether or not to vote to separate from England, a formal declaration of independence should be prepared. Five delegates were selected to prepare the document: Benjamin Franklin, Thomas Jefferson, Roger Sherman, Robert Livingston, and John Adams.

Thomas Jefferson was ultimately selected to write the first draft of the declaration. He created his first draft, then presented it to the committee. They suggested changes and deletions. Then they waited.

INDEPENDENCE DAY

On July 1, 1776, the day finally arrived for the delegates to cast their votes—for or against independence. It was not an easy decision. John Dickinson of Pennsylvania argued earnestly that it was too early to decide to separate from Britain. Adams then rose to make the case for independence. It would be remembered by many of the delegates attending the conference as the single most important speech ever given in the Congress; Richard Stockton, the delegate from New Jersey, described Adams afterwards as "the man to whom the country is most indebted for the great measure of independency. "

As the day drew to a close, an informal vote was called.

Nine colonies voted for independence; Pennsylvania and South Carolina voted against. New York abstained, and the two delegates from Delaware split on the issue, making it impossible for that colony to cast a deciding vote. When the group from South Carolina suggested that the formal vote be delayed for one day to see if a unanimous decision could be reached, nearly everyone agreed.

That night was spent in intense debate and discussion. A rider was quickly sent on horseback to bring back to Philadelphia the third member of Delaware's delegation, who was sick in bed. He arrived on the following day, and the final decision—a decision that would transform life in the colonies—was quickly reached. With the third delegate present to break the tie, Delaware voted for independence. Pennsylvania changed its vote to support independence. South Carolina also changed its vote. In all, 12 colonies voted for independence. Only New York abstained.

At the end of the day, John Adams wrote a joyful letter to Abigail, noting somewhat incorrectly that July 2 would be remembered as the greatest day in American history, a day for thanksgiving and celebration.

On July 3 and 4, the Declaration of Independence was officially presented and debated. Some 30 changes were made to the draft, cutting about one-fourth of the document. Then the debate ended and once more, 12 colonies voted for independence while New York abstained.

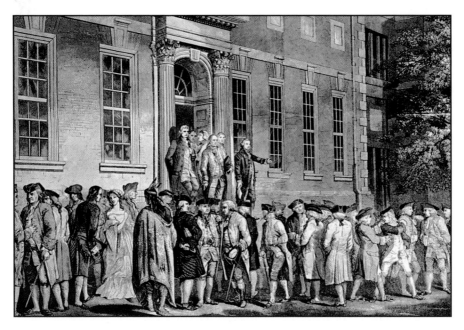

Members of the Second Continental Congress emerge from Independence Hall, Philadelphia, after finalizing the Declaration of Independence on July 4, 1776. Thomas Jefferson wrote the first draft, which then underwent many changes. After several votes, 12 colonies were in favor of independence (New York abstained).

MISSION TO FRANCE

Adams was given the challenging task of serving as the chairman of the Board of War and Ordnance, the committee responsible for overseeing military operations. The Continental Army was in desperate need of funding for supplies, clothes, food, and new recruits, and Adams was forced to balance these needs with the limited funds available to a congress that had no nation to tax.

As Adams wrestled with these critical problems, he received sad news. Abigail had given birth, but the little girl was stillborn.

Given these pressures, it is not surprising that, by November 1777, John Adams had decided to return home to Massachusetts and refused to serve another term in Congress. The small sum he was receiving for his work was barely enough to cover his expenses. His law practice and farm were in disarray, and he missed his family.

But on November 28, 1777, Adams learned that he, along with Benjamin Franklin and Arthur Lee, had been chosen to represent their countrymen in a mission to France. Adams believed that it was critical to form an alliance with France, but a voyage across the ocean was no easy matter in those days, and one made during wartime was even more hazardous. Ultimately, he agreed to make the voyage, and decided to take along his 10-year-old son, John Quincy. They arrived on the deck of their ship, the *Boston,* on February 13, 1778, but strong winds prevented the ship from sailing for nearly two days.

The voyage across the Atlantic Ocean lasted for nearly six weeks. The *Boston* was chased by a British ship for two days. A four-day-long storm rocked the vessel, and the main mast cracked above and below deck. On four occasions, their own ship pursued British ships, one of which it captured. Finally, the *Boston* arrived in France.

In the small Parisian suburb of Passy, Adams joined the other members of the delegation. He was disturbed to learn that, some 10 days before he had left his home, France and America had signed treaties of alliance and commerce. The treaty of commerce was acceptable on all points; the treaty of alliance was less satisfactory, as it gave no deadline for

In November 1777, John Adams decided to quit his political career in Congress in order to return to his family and his law practice. Later that month, however, he learned that he and two other men had been appointed to represent the United States on a mission to garner French support, which was considered crucial for colonial independence.

France's entry into the war. But these treaties left little for Adams and his fellow commissioners to do, and the little that needed to be done caused deep divisions among the three. The deepest divisions were between Lee and Franklin. The commission's paperwork was in disorder: no copies of official documents had been kept, and there were no records of expenses or negotiations. Adams set to work, trying to bring order out of the chaos.

Finally, frustrated at the inefficiency and disagreements between his fellow commissioners, Adams wrote to Congress, suggesting that one commissioner would be more sensible than three. Congress agreed and, to Adams' disappointment, selected Franklin as the sole commissioner. After 10 months in France, Adams and his son returned to Massachusetts in May 1779.

A BRIEF STAY

Shortly after his return to Braintree, Adams was elected to serve as the representative to Massachusetts' Constitutional Convention. Adams was one of 313 delegates who assembled in Cambridge in September to draft a constitution for the convention, and he was soon chosen to write this important document. Adams' draft, with minor alterations, became the final version that was adopted in 1780. It remains in force in Massachusetts today, and is important for its emphasis on a strong executive branch (rather than the stronger legislative branches that other colonies had created) and its system of checks and balances marked by independent, popularly elected judges. These ideas would later be copied by the drafters of the United States Constitution.

Even as Adams was putting the finishing touches on Massachusetts' constitution, Congress elected him to serve as "minister plenipotentiary" to negotiate a peace treaty with Great Britain. It was clear that this would be a lengthy mission—peace was still far off. But Adams agreed; he understood that it was an important task, and he also welcomed the opportunity for a diplomatic mission that might prove more satisfactory than the one he had undertaken to France.

Adams, with two private secretaries and two of his sons, nine-year-old Charles and 12-year-old John Quincy, set sail on November 14, 1779. He had been home from France for only 71 days.

DIPLOMAT IN EUROPE

Adams crossed the Atlantic in a brisk 23 days, landing in Spain when the ship sprang a leak. The ship could not be quickly repaired, so Adams and his companions were forced to travel to Paris by land. Much of the trip was made on mules, and the group traveled slowly from one Spanish village to another, sleeping in beds infested with fleas and lice. Finally, three months after setting out from Spain, they arrived in Paris.

Paris was to serve as Adams' base while he negotiated with Britain. In fact, Adams was instructed to work through the French government, to inform both France and Britain of what the Americans wanted. Much of Adams' negotiating was carried out with Charles Gravier, the Comte de Vergennes, who served as King Louis XVI's adviser on foreign affairs. Vergennes had no wish to see the Americans successfully negotiate a commercial treaty with England, and he employed several tactics to delay Adams' efforts.

Benjamin Franklin had traveled to France with John Adams and Arthur Lee in 1777. Adams had dealt unsuccessfully with Charles Gravier, Louis XVI's adviser on foreign affairs. Adams became impatient with Vergennes' continued stalling. Franklin eventually became the primary American ambassador to France.

Finally, after several months of Vergennes' stalling tactics, Adams grew impatient and wrote a letter insisting that France must send additional ships to America to meet its promise under the treaty of alliance. Vergennes claimed to be insulted and said that he would no longer deal with

Adams, and instead would deal only with Benjamin Franklin. He forwarded all of the letters Adams had written to him to Franklin.

Adams, deciding that there was little he could accomplish in Paris, took his sons and traveled to the Netherlands in the summer of 1780. Congress soon appointed him to serve as the temporary minister to the Netherlands, with the goal of negotiating treaties with the Dutch.

The task was not an easy one. The Netherlands had a treaty with Britain, and when the English learned of Adams' efforts, they sent ships to attack the Dutch. As Adams worked to sort out the complications, he learned that Congress had responded to Vergennes' complaints and appointed four other peace commissioners to join Adams in France (including Franklin), and that the entire peace commission would be forced to consult and report to Vergennes himself.

It was almost too much for Adams, who became quite ill. But by October 1781 welcome news came—combined French and American forces had successfully beaten the British army at Yorktown in Virginia. On October 19, the British surrendered. The successes gave Adams' mission a new purpose, and he began to lobby the Netherlands to officially recognize the government of the new nation. His hard work eventually paid off, and a treaty of friendship and commerce was signed. Adams was also able to negotiate loans of $3.5 million with several Dutch banks—loans that brought critical assistance to the American cause.

Adams then returned to France, where he joined the

other American representatives. Franklin argued strongly that they should follow their instructions from Congress and consult with the French in any peace negotiations with England; another commissioner, John Jay, felt that no other nation should be given the right to control American diplomacy. Adams agreed with Jay.

Negotiations were complicated because of an earlier treaty signed with France. According to the terms of that treaty, the American delegation could not finalize peace terms with England until England and France had also reached a peace agreement. The negotiating dragged on for several months, disgusting and disappointing Adams. Finally, a peace treaty between England and America was concluded on September 3, 1783. On that same date, additional treaties were signed between England, Spain and France—these treaties essentially divided the territory of North America among the 13 former colonies, Britain, and Spain.

With the treaties concluded and the war ended, Adams felt safe in asking his family to join him. Abigail and their daughter, Nabby, arrived in England in July 1784, and the three traveled to Paris together.

For the next several months, Abigail enjoyed Paris while John continued negotiating the fine points of a trade agreement. He hoped to be named America's first minister to Great Britain. In February 1785, his wish was granted, and three months later he left for England.

4

DIPLOMACY
AND POLITICS

JOHN ADAMS WAS 49 years old when he traveled to England to assume his new post as minister to Great Britain. The prospect of paying his first official visit to England's King George III made him nervous. He had played a critical role in the war that had separated America from England; now he had come as the first official ambassador of the new nation. When he finally met the king, Adams expressed the wish of his country to build a new relationship with England, one based on friendship. The king replied that he regretted being unable to prevent America from separating from England, but he too agreed that friendship should be their new goal. The king then bowed, and the meeting was over.

John Adams (left) met with King George III of England (right) in his post as minister to Great Britain, which he assumed in 1784 and held for three years. The men agreed to work toward building a friendship between the two countries. Adams enjoyed this post because it allowed him to escape the difficulties in France and to spend time with his family.

For the next three years, Adams served as America's chief diplomat in England. It was a happy period. Abigail and John were together, and John was relieved to be away from the intrigue of Vergennes and the French.

But he faced a difficult task: trying to address the remaining problems of the Revolutionary War. Many of the diplomats he encountered in England treated him coldly, displaying little interest in reestablishing ties with a country they once ruled. There were strong anti-American feelings in England, and Adams felt that his goals—achieving a period of peace for America and rebuilding trade between England and her former colonies—might prove impossible.

Adams' task was made more difficult by the fact that there was no central authority in the nation that he was representing. The colonies were now states, but each of the states was setting up its own guidelines for trade—if Massachusetts banned British goods from coming in to Boston Harbor, the British would simply negotiate a deal with a different state and send their goods to America via that route.

In fact, there was little that the new country could do as a single, unified nation. It could negotiate peace (or declare war) and set up an army or navy; it could send out ambassadors and receive them from other nations; it could make treaties. But it could not pay its debts, collect taxes, or even create and enforce its own laws.

A NEW NATION

By 1788, it was clear to Adams that his mission could not succeed, and he asked Congress to accept his resignation. His request was finally granted, and in April, he and Abigail sailed for home, leaving behind their daughter, son-in-law ("Nabby" had married while in England), and new grandson.

Adams was greeted like a hero upon his arrival in Boston. Cannons thundered and church bells rang out. The Adamses had purchased a new home, and soon they set about overseeing needed repairs. John was offered many important positions and was elected, once more, to serve as a representative in Congress. He refused, saying that he wished instead to settle back into life as a private citizen.

It did not take long for him to change his mind. Within a month after his arrival, pleased at the hero's welcome he had received upon his return, he decided what he wanted his next job to be: he wanted to become vice president of the United Sates. By this time, all of the states had ratified the Constitution and the nation's new name had been universally adopted.

THE VICE PRESIDENCY

When the position of president of the United States was created, there was little doubt about who would be the first man to hold that office—it would be George Washington. But the question of who would serve as vice president sparked more debate. The governor of Massachusetts, Alexander Hamilton, had hoped to be chosen, as had the governor of New York, George Clinton. John Jay, a former diplomat to France, was also a candidate.

It is important to remember that the system for electing a president and vice president as originally created by the Constitutional Convention was quite different from the system we know today. There were no political parties, and candidates did not travel from place to place campaigning or trying to win votes. Instead, the man receiving the most electoral votes (from electors selected in each state to form the electoral college) would become president; the first runner-up would become vice president. To make things even more complicated, each of the 69 electors was required to vote twice. They could not cast their

PRESIDENT ADAMS' LEGACY

The Right Men at the Right Moment

At two critical points in America's history, John Adams made an important contribution—not through his own actions, but by his willingness to support someone else for the task at hand. Adams was an astute observer of others and of himself, and he was well aware of the strengths and weaknesses of the men around him.

In May 1775, at the Second Continental Congress in Philadelphia, Adams understood that his fellow delegates were divided about the conflict taking shape in the colonies. Many still clung to the hope that the king and England's Parliament could be negotiated with; still others felt that independence from England was the only solution.

On June 14, 1775, John Adams stood up to nominate a member of the Virginia delegation to serve as commander in chief of the Continental Army. He named George Washington, knowing that Washington would be a unifying presence, representing the largest colony (Virginia) and the South. He would make it clear that the rebellion was not merely a Massachusetts conflict. Washington had impressed Adams with his willingness to risk his fortune in the conflict, and he had demonstrated his leadership skills during the French and Indian War. Adams also appreciated Washington's two votes for the same candidate, but instead had to vote for two different men.

Because John Adams was so popular, there was some concern that perhaps there might be a tie—many of the electors might cast their first vote for George Washington and their second vote for John Adams. In the event of a tie, the House of Representatives would be forced to decide who would be president, and some felt this would be embarrassing for George Washington and make the choice for president seem uncertain.

quiet care in discussing the conflict. He never grew overly passionate or excited, and Adams was certain that Washington would appreciate the enormity of the task facing him and be worthy of the new post.

One year later, Adams would once more show skill at helping to assign the right man to the right task. In June of 1776, the delegates at the Second Continental Congress were debating whether or not to vote for independence. A committee was formed to draft a declaration of independence—a committee that included both Jefferson and Adams. In later years, Adams claimed that Jefferson had suggested that Adams should draft the document, but that he had insisted Jefferson be the author. Adams argued that Jefferson was a better writer and, as a Virginian, would be the better political choice to serve as the document's chief author.

Jefferson would disagree with this version, but it is certain that Adams, as the more senior delegate, might well have argued for the right to serve as author himself. Instead, he supported Jefferson in his efforts, adding a few editorial suggestions to the final document, but contributing to what became an important step in the revolution by his willingness to play a supporting role.

Alexander Hamilton of New York, a leading political figure, was determined to make sure that this did not happen. He liked John Adams, but felt that to strengthen the new country the choice for president must be clear and unanimous. Hamilton worked behind the scenes to make sure that some of the electors did not cast their second vote for Adams.

In the end, George Washington was the unanimous choice for president. John Adams finished second and, at the age of 53, became the first vice president of the United States.

Adams, although disappointed that he had won less than half of the electoral votes, was still pleased to have been named to the second highest office in the country. As he left for the nation's new capital of New York, he was given a grand send-off. On April 13, 1789, he set out from Braintree, accompanied by cavalry. When he reached Boston, crowds greeted him, cannons sounded, and more than 40 carriages escorted him from the city. He was cheered as he traveled south through New England. When he arrived at the tip of Manhattan, late on the afternoon of April 20, he was met by another cavalry troop, several members of Congress, and a group of private citizens who escorted him into the city that was to become his new home.

A NEW BEGINNING

Despite the grand scale of the celebrations, Adams worried about the new chapter he was beginning. The United States had no history of joining together, and many dangerous divisions were already becoming clear. Many

Americans had resisted the idea of a union of states, feeling their primary loyalty only to the state in which they lived. Indeed, two political groups had formed to express these concerns: the Federalists, who wanted a strong central government, and the anti-Federalists (later known as Democratic-Republicans), who believed that the states should remain strong and any central government should have as little power as possible over states' rights.

Adams was also worried by a very basic concern— money. New York was expensive, and Adams was not sure where he and Abigail would live or what salary he would earn. George Washington had argued that public officials should serve without pay, but he was a very wealthy man. Adams disagreed, noting that this approach meant that only the wealthiest men would be able to serve in any public capacity. He felt that government officials should be paid a salary in keeping with their responsibilities and could only hope that Congress (and Washington) would ultimately agree.

"Public business, my son, must always be done by somebody. . . . If wise men decline it, others will not; if honest men refuse it, others will not. A young man should weigh well his plans. . . . His first maxim then should be to place his honor out of reach of all men. In order to do this he must make it a rule never to become dependent on public employments for subsistence. Let him have a trade, a profession, a farm, a shop, something where he can honestly live, and then he may engage in public affairs, if invited, upon independent principles."

— When John Adams was serving as vice president, his son Thomas wrote him a letter indicating that he, too, would like a career in government service. Adams' response noted his own beliefs about the ideal public servant.

On April 21, John Adams was officially received at the door of the Federal Hall building, the place where Congress met, and was then escorted upstairs to the Senate. There was no official "swearing-in" ceremony; instead the new vice president was simply greeted and led to his chair at the front of the room. Adams gave a brief speech, noting that he "cheerfully and readily" accepted the duties of vice president.

The job Adams was assuming had been given only a sketchy description in the new Constitution, which noted that the vice president would serve as president of the Senate, but would have no vote unless a tie-breaking vote needed to be cast. It was a somewhat ceremonial role, not terribly well suited to a man who loved debate and argument and immersed himself deeply in every task he undertook.

But Adams determined to focus quickly on matters of procedure—whether or not, for example, the Senate should stand or remain seated when the president spoke before them. Washington arrived for his inauguration two days later, surrounded by cheering crowds. Adams was once more linked to the man he had nominated to serve as commander in chief of the Continental Army. He was charged with formally welcoming the president and escorting him to the front of the Senate. Adams then stood by Washington's side as he repeated the oath of office.

It was not long into his first term as vice president that Adams was criticized for his emphasis on ceremony.

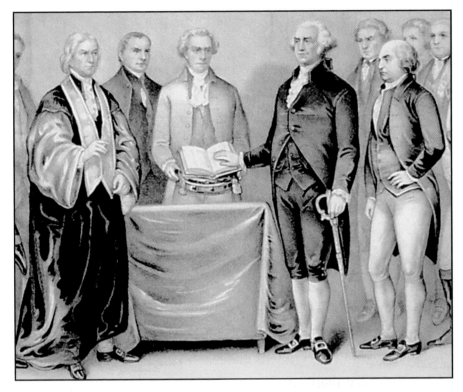

Several men, including John Adams, had been candidates for the first presidency, but George Washington was the unanimous choice. Adams, standing to the right of George Washington, was the runner-up and thus became the first vice president of the United States.

Adams believed that the United States must be viewed as a strong and powerful nation, as mighty and impressive as those of the great nations of Europe. In order for America's leaders to be considered equal to the leaders of the European nations, and to impress upon American citizens the importance of a strong central government, Adams felt that the titles used to address the government's leaders should reflect great dignity and respect. For a month, the Senate debated such matters as whether the president should be addressed as "Excellency," "His Majesty the President," or even the wordy "His Highness the President of the United States of America and Protector of the Rights of the Same."

It was the first sign that Adams' time in Europe had left him unaware of the changes that had taken place in America. He spent far too much time arguing for the importance of symbolic distinctions when the mood of the nation favored simpler ideals. Some began to label Adams a monarchist (someone who supported a government ruled by a king or queen). One member of Congress, noting Adams' stout shape, suggested that he be given the honorary title "His Rotundity," and the nickname soon spread. Adams struggled with the hands-off approach he was supposed to exercise in the Senate, and instead, frequently occupied the Senate's time with lectures and discussions that annoyed nearly everyone.

The vice president was occasionally called in to discuss national business with George Washington, but Adams found that the president was rarely influenced by the opinions of others. Washington's cabinet included Alexander Hamilton as secretary of the treasury and Thomas Jefferson as secretary of state. Both men held strong—and quite different—opinions about how the new nation should be governed, and their disagreements would dramatically weaken Washington's administration.

REVOLUTION IN FRANCE

The news soon reached America that a revolution had taken place in France. The French people had stormed the Parisian prison, the Bastille, set all of its prisoners free, and had then cut off the head of its commander and carried it through the streets of Paris, dripping blood. Violent mobs were raging throughout the city, leaving destruction wherever they went.

For most Americans, the news of a revolution in France was greeted joyfully. France had stood beside America in its fight for liberty; now the French people seemed to be following America's example.

But Adams was not one of those who celebrated the news of the French Revolution. He was concerned by the reports of violence, of angry mobs taking over Paris, and quickly began work on a series of newspaper essays that criticized the events in France and reminded Americans that a government with checks and balances was the only kind that could maintain peace and security.

Adams' essays sparked an immediate outcry. Once more he was out of step with the rest of the country, and he made the mistake of demonstrating it on paper. Once again, he was labeled a monarchist and an enemy of the ordinary citizen.

The essays also served to demonstrate the growing split within Washington's administration. Adams and Hamilton, supporters of a strong central government, found themselves in opposition to Thomas Jefferson and others, who believed that the states should retain certain

The French Revolution of 1789 in part followed the ideals of the American Revolution. Many Americans, including Thomas Jefferson, supported the people of France, but Adams was concerned by the riots and violence. This disagreement was the beginning of the split between Adams and Jefferson, who had been friends for many years.

powers for themselves. These men were outspoken in their support of the French Revolution as an example of the rights of ordinary men to govern themselves.

It was a particularly painful split between Adams and Jefferson, old friends who had served together in the

Continental Congress and in Europe, and who now served the country under George Washington. Jefferson's concern was that Adams' vision of America would create a country that was merely a copy of England, rather than the dramatically different nation that Jefferson wanted it to become. The two did not argue or discuss these issues in person; instead, they published their thoughts in letters, in books, and in newspaper articles. These writings were critical to shaping America, reflecting the ideas and hopes of those who first led the nation, but the debates that followed were often harsh and bitter.

In the summer of 1790, two matters occupied Congress: first, where the new national capital was to be located and, second, whether or not the federal government would take over payment of the war debts each state had accumulated during the Revolutionary War. Those in the north favored keeping the capital where it was—in New York—or as a compromise, relocating it to Philadelphia. They argued strongly that the national government should help assume some of the war debts that were crippling their states' economies. Those in the south felt that the new nation could not be fairly represented by a capital so far north. They argued strongly against a change in the war debt policy, as many of the southern states had already paid off their war debts.

The two issues soon became linked, and a compromise was gradually worked out. If the southern states supported the national government taking over the war debts, the capital would be located in the south, along the Potomac River. In the meantime, the capital would be temporarily located in Philadelphia for the next 10 years until a new capital could be constructed.

By late fall, the Adams family (along with the rest of the government) had relocated to Philadelphia. Adams had always loved the city, and he and Abigail were happy to find themselves once more among friends. But the split with Jefferson and others weighed heavily on him as the time for a new national election drew near.

Washington had indicated that he wanted to step down from office after his first term. He expressed his displeasure with the growing split in his cabinet; he was tired of the demands of the presidency and disgusted with the criticisms of a press that was increasingly influenced by one group of politicians or another. The country showed signs of splitting into two groups. The Federalists, led by Alexander Hamilton, supported a strong national government; the Democratic-Republicans, represented by Thomas Jefferson, championed the rights of individual states.

Although Hamilton and Jefferson were divided on nearly every issue, they did agree on one point: Washington must stay on to serve a second term, or the divisions might lead to a civil war. While Washington was clearly once more the unanimous choice for president, John Adams' candidacy was not so obvious. In fact, there were several candidates for vice president, and Adams found himself the target of frequent criticism in the press as someone who was trying to prepare "the people of America for a King and nobility."

By November 1792, Washington had agreed to serve for a second term. Despite the attacks against Adams, he was the final choice for vice president, winning 77 electoral votes.

5

THE BURDENS
OF OFFICE

JOHN ADAMS BEGAN his second term as vice president in 1793. Living alone in Philadelphia (Abigail had returned home to Massachusetts), he set up a quiet daily routine that included reading the newspapers, going to the Senate, visiting with friends, attending church on Sundays, and writing letters to his family.

Adams had come to understand that the office of vice president offered little to an ambitious man. He wrote to Abigail, "My country in its wisdom contrived for me that most insignificant office that ever the invention of man contrived or his imagination conceived."

John Adams began a second term as Washington's vice president in 1793. He soon realized that the job offered few challenges and little to do. Around this time, he began writing to Thomas Jefferson, after Jefferson left the government for his estate in Virginia. The resumed friendship would not last long.

In December 1793, Thomas Jefferson left Washington's administration and moved to Monticello, his estate near Charlottesville, Virgina. Adams wrote him a brief note, congratulating him on his decision to spend spring far from the "din of politics and rumors of war," and the two former friends soon found themselves exchanging letters on safe topics.

In May 1794, Adams received the welcome news that Washington was nominating his son, John Quincy Adams, to serve as minister to the Netherlands—a position that Adams himself had held many years earlier. Adams presided over the Senate when it confirmed his son's nomination.

During much of Adams' second term as vice president, the country was influenced by events overseas. The developments in France continued to spark debate—the French Revolution had led to the Reign of Terror, with the guillotine claiming the lives of the French king and countless French aristocrats.

When France unexpectedly declared war on England and the Netherlands, the American government was forced to consider its position in the conflict. A war was certain to affect American trade with England, trade critical to the American economy. But America was also bound by treaty to France. Washington decided that the United States would remain neutral in the conflict, and Adams supported him in this unpopular choice.

A NEW ELECTION

By 1796, Washington had made it clear that he would not seek a third term as president, and speculation was growing about who would succeed him. John Adams was 60 years old, experiencing some of the discomforts of aging and well aware that any man who succeeded Washington would suffer from comparison with the great hero. He was tired of politics, yet not sure that he wanted to do anything else.

Adams requested a leave of absence, and traveled home in May. For several months, he simply enjoyed working on the farm, helping to build a new barn, cutting down trees, and threshing hay.

It was a happy time, but it did not last. On September 17, newspapers published the official announcement that George Washington planned to retire, as well as the text of his farewell address. The country was quickly launched into a new era: two political parties with two opposing candidates sought the office of president. John Adams was the choice for Federalists; Thomas Jefferson was favored by the Democratic-Republicans.

As bitter debate and critical press coverage erupted, the two leading candidates remained at their homes in Virginia and Massachusetts, doing their best not to be personally drawn into the fierce battle. Adams was again criticized for being the friend of kings and royalty. He was also accused of plotting to overthrow the government, of wanting to create a monarchy so that his son, John Quincy Adams, could succeed him in ruling the country. Jefferson was treated every bit as roughly. Federalist papers accused him of being a coward and an atheist.

John Adams finally returned to Philadelphia on December 2, 1796. Congress met three days later. Presidential politics was the leading topic among the representatives of the now-16 states (Vermont, Kentucky, and Tennessee had joined the union). Alexander Hamilton was involved in a last minute, behind-the-scenes effort to shift votes away from Adams and over to a candidate Hamilton believed he could influence. By February 8, 1797, the results of the electoral ballots were read. John Adams had won the election by a total of three electoral votes, receiving 71 to Thomas Jefferson's 68.

FAREWELL TO THE CHIEF

On March 4, 1797, House and Senate members, Supreme Court justices, and many other government officials, all gathered in Philadelphia to witness the inauguration of the second president of the United States. First to appear on the dais was George Washington, who was greeted with enthusiastic applause. Then came the new vice president, Thomas Jefferson. Finally, the new president, John Adams, appeared.

Adams chose to begin his presidency in a simple manner, perhaps hoping to prove false those critics who had labeled him a monarchist. In contrast with Washington, who had arrived for his inauguration in a grand carriage drawn by six white horses, Adams rode to his inauguration in a simple carriage pulled by only two horses. The two Virginians who stood on the dais with him—Washington and Jefferson—were tall and elegantly dressed. Adams provided a severe contrast; the shorter, stouter man was dressed only in a simple suit of gray cloth with no fancy buttons or buckles. But his inaugural speech made clear

John Adams, a Federalist, was elected to the presidency in 1797, after a bitter battle with Thomas Jefferson, who represented the Democratic-Republicans. Both men were sharply criticized in the press, and in the end, Adams barely won: He received three more electoral votes than Jefferson.

his strong feelings about the country he was charged with leading, his appreciation of the current system of government, and his support for states' rights.

After the speech ended, many in the audience seemed deeply moved. But Adams was convinced that it was the fact that Washington was leaving office that had moved many to tears. In fact, Adams later wrote, Washington's face was the only one that seemed untroubled on that day. "Me thought I heard him think, 'Ay! I am fairly out and you are fairly in! See which of us will be the happiest!'"

For the next week, President Adams stayed at the Francis Hotel while the Washingtons slowly moved their things from Philadelphia's President's House. Washington visited Adams several times and hosted a dinner in Adams' honor. Still later, he met with Adams to see if he might be interested in purchasing some of the furniture that Washington had bought when he was president and Adams bought a few of the pieces.

On March 9, George Washington and his family rode out from Philadelphia quietly, with no ceremonies to mark

> "... There can be no spectacle presented by any nation more pleasing, more noble, majestic, or august than an assembly like that which has so often been seen in this and the other chamber of Congress; of a government in which the executive authority, as well as that of all the branches of the legislature, are exercised by citizens selected at regular periods by their neighbors, to make and execute laws for the general good. . . . For it is the people only that are represented; it is their power and majesty that is reflected, and only for their good, in every legitimate government, under whatever form it may appear. . . ."
>
> — On March 4, 1797, John Adams became the second president of the United States. In his inaugural speech, given before the House and Senate, he attempted to end some of the bitter division that had marked the election and spoke of his own commitment to government of the people, by the people, and for the people.

the occasion, and Adams moved into the President's House. Adams was expected to pay rent while living in the grand mansion—$225 per month—and to oversee the cleanup of the house following the Washingtons' departure. He was forced to pay for his own carriage and horses, his own china and glasses, his own kitchen utensils and linens—all on a salary of some $25,000 per year. He warned his wife that the family's finances would be very tight.

Even before the inauguration, Adams had made a decision that would prove perhaps the worst of his presidency. Rather than choosing his own cabinet, he had decided to keep the four department heads Washington had chosen in his second term. These were Attorney General Charles Lee, Secretary of State Timothy Pickering, Secretary of the Treasury Oliver Wolcott, and Secretary of War James McHenry. Pickering, Wolcott, and McHenry were all younger than Adams; they were all Federalists and were strongly anti-French and pro-British, like their mentor, Alexander Hamilton. Hamilton had returned to his law practice in New York, but through these cabinet members, he intended to strongly influence the national government.

Adams also found little support from his vice president, Thomas Jefferson. At the time of the inauguration, Adams and Thomas Jefferson had met and discussed what they believed to be the most pressing concerns facing them. But the spirit of bipartisan cooperation soon faded. It is difficult to imagine how a president and vice president who had competed in an election could ever have been expected to work together, but at least Washington had benefited from Adams' loyalty and support. Adams could not expect the same from Jefferson, who was from a different party and had different views on many important matters of policy.

FOREIGN AFFAIRS

Almost immediately, Adams was forced to focus on foreign policy. France had begun seizing American ships in an attempt to block trade between America and England. The French government had refused to meet with the new American minister to France, General Charles Pinckney, and war with France seemed almost certain.

Adams met with Congress to propose a series of defensive measures that might help avoid war. He wanted to create a strong navy to protect American ships against seizure, increase the size of the cavalry and artillery, and pass new laws to organize and arm the militia to help defend the country. He also made a new attempt at negotiating with the French, appointing three men to serve as peace envoys. Adams was determined to negotiate an agreement with France and felt it important that both parties be represented in the mission. He specifically selected Elbridge Gerry of Massachusetts, a Democratic-Republican, as one of his envoys.

Nearly a year passed before any word was received from the envoys. In the meantime, Adams' administration suffered nearly constant attacks. There were no restrictions on what newspapers printed in those days, and most focused more on publishing opinions than actual news. Most of the opinions published did not support the president.

John Adams' decision to appoint his son, John Quincy, as minister to Prussia sparked fiercely critical editorials, claiming that the posting to Berlin offered proof that Adams intended to use his presidency to make a fortune for himself and his family. Adams had consulted Washington before making the appointment, and Washington had approved the decision, praising John Quincy for his diplomatic skill, but the editorials were damaging. Additional criticism followed John Quincy's decision to marry Louisa Catherine Johnson, a young woman whose father was American and whose mother was English. The Democratic-Republicans claimed that Adams was thrilled that his son was marrying an "English lady."

XYZ AFFAIR

The American peace envoys arrived in Paris in October 1797. They were kept waiting for several days, and finally, were given only 15 minutes to meet with French Foreign Minister Talleyrand. A few days later, they were approached by three men who claimed to be secret agents from Talleyrand. These agents told the American envoys

This political cartoon depicts American resistance to threats and demands for money from the French in the XYZ Affair. At the time, the United States was on the brink of war with France, and knowledge of the extortion attempts led to Congressional approval for Adams' proposals to increase national defense, including fortifying harbors and creating a navy.

that Talleyrand was inclined to help the United States, but that a bribe of $250,000 to Talleyrand and a loan of $10 million to the Republic of France would certainly help him make up his mind.

The Americans refused to negotiate and wrote up reports of the meetings—reports that finally reached the president in March 1798. The reports referred to the three French agents as "X, Y, and Z." Adams knew how damaging this information would be to his effort to hold America back from the brink of war with France. In his initial report on the diplomatic mission to Congress, he said only that the mission had failed. But Congress insisted on reading the envoys' correspondence, and the "X, Y, Z dispatches" were released.

Many Democratic-Republicans in Congress who had demanded to see the documents had done so in the belief that Adams was trying to create a crisis where there was none. The documents clearly proved that what was happening in France was much worse than Adams had suggested. Congress soon passed the measures Adams recommended for increased national defense. A Navy Department, separate from the War Department, was created, and a fleet was authorized. A "provisional army" of some 10,000 men was approved, and money was put into the budget for artillery and to fortify harbors.

NATURALIZATION, ALIEN, AND SEDITION ACTS

The country seemed to rally behind the president as the nation prepared for war. But Adams did not ask Congress to declare war on France. Instead, he asked it to focus on enemies that might be waiting on America's own soil. There was great suspicion and fear of foreigners, particularly French immigrants, who might be acting as enemy agents. To help address these concerns, Congress passed the Naturalization, Alien, and Sedition Acts in 1798.

The two Alien Acts gave the president a power that had previously been granted to the states—the power to expel any foreigners that he thought might be "dangerous." Contained within the Alien Acts was a Naturalization Act, which extended from five to fourteen years the period of time necessary for a foreigner to live on American soil before he could be granted citizenship.

But the act that sparked the most controversy was the Sedition Act. According to the terms of this act, anyone who was guilty of "false, scandalous and malicious" writing against the president, Congress or government in an attempt to stir up sedition (rebellion against the government) faced a fine or imprisonment. The Federalists, who supported this act, claimed that it was a necessary measure in times of war, despite the fact that it seemed a violation of the Constitution's protection of free speech. Several newspapermen were quickly convicted under the new law—nearly all of them Democratic-Republican editors.

PRESIDENT ADAMS' LEGACY

Sedition Act of 1798

In 1798, as the prospect of war with France loomed, legislation was passed to address national concerns about enemies that might be hiding within America's borders. The Alien and Naturalization Acts extended the period of time necessary before foreigners could be granted citizenship. They also gave President John Adams the right to expel any foreign-born people he felt might be a threat to America's security.

The Sedition Act of 1798 was even more controversial. In apparent conflict with the freedom of speech rights spelled out in the Constitution, the Sedition Act made it a crime to criticize the president, his administration, or Congress. Those who broke this law could be fined or imprisoned.

It quickly became clear that the Sedition Act was a tool being used to silence any opposition to President Adams' administration. More than a dozen journalists were prosecuted, nearly all of them critics of Adams.

MILITARY MATTERS

On July 2, 1798, the House took the noteworthy step of passing its first direct tax on American citizens, a tax on land designed to help pay for the cost of increased military expenses. On that same date, John Adams announced his choice for commander in chief of the new provisional army: George Washington.

Washington agreed and Congress appointed him, but discussions about who would serve as Washington's second in command revealed deep divisions between Adams and his cabinet. Given Washington's age and poor health, it was clear that this was a critical position, not one that could be filled without serious consideration.

While Adams did not draft the legislation himself, he clearly supported its passage, and was grateful for its ability to silence the critics who had attacked his personal and professional life.

But his gratitude would prove shortsighted. Public anger against the crackdown on the press was widespread. The Sedition Act would expire in 1801, but Adams' presidency would expire sooner. Opponents of Adams used the Sedition Act as evidence of the president's willingness to ignore the Constitution and the rights of "ordinary people" to express their opinions freely. In 1800, this argument helped to contribute to Adams' defeat in the presidential election. Future presidents would remember the successes and failures of the Alien, Naturalization, and Sedition Acts of 1798 whenever faced with concerns about national security.

Alexander Hamilton desperately wanted the number-two position, but Adams, knowing how Hamilton had betrayed him before, refused to appoint him. Hamilton, however, had Washington's support. He also had the support of three members of Adams' cabinet. After months of arguing, Adams was forced to give in and nominate Hamilton for the post.

Hamilton quickly mapped out a grand campaign, one in marked contrast to Adams' desire for peace through strength. The new Inspector General, as he was now titled, talked of leading an American army into foreign-held territories in Louisiana, New Orleans, Florida and Mexico.

Meanwhile, Adams was receiving hints that France might want peace. Publicly, the president spoke in strong language about preparing for war; in private, he kept open the option of negotiating. His hopes were answered when he received a letter from Talleyrand, indicating that a minister from the United States, one with the mission of attempting to resolve the differences that had arisen between the two nations, would be welcomed in France.

On February 18, 1799, President Adams delivered Talleyrand's letter to Congress, along with a proposal for renewed negotiations with France and a suggestion for a new minister. Members of Congress were shocked: American ships were being attacked by French vessels, Hamilton was drafting plans for a great army, and now Adams wanted to try again to negotiate? When Adams was asked to withdraw his nomination of the new peace envoy, he refused.

No one wanted to speak out publicly in favor of war, but the president's move infuriated Hamilton and created an even deeper split between Adams' own cabinet and the Federalists. Adams had done the unthinkable. He had acted independently, disregarding the wishes of his own party and those of many of his countrymen.

6

PRESIDENTIAL POLITICS

THE DEATH OF George Washington on December 14, 1799, briefly shifted the country's focus away from internal squabbling and the prospect of war. Washington had once more unified the country—this time in grief. But as America mourned, its leaders continued to disagree.

Almost immediately, Adams made it clear that he would not appoint Hamilton to replace Washington as commander in chief. The American envoys (the mission had grown from one diplomat to three) arrived in France and were welcomed both by Talleyrand and France's new leader, Napoleon Bonaparte. The envoys returned to America with a commercial treaty, one that spelled peace for both sides.

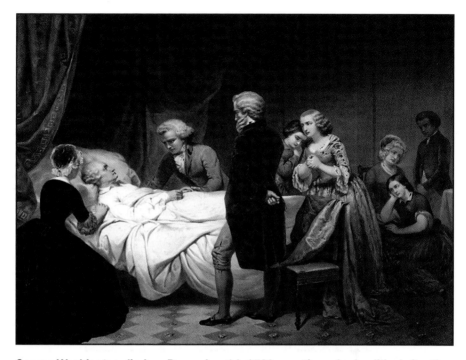

George Washington died on December 14, 1799, creating a bad political situation for Adams. Adams refused to nominate Alexander Hamilton as the new commander in chief, worsening his relationship with Hamilton, who was a powerful Federalist. Many Federalists believed that Adams was abandoning them, creating a split in the party that allowed the Democratic-Republicans to win the next election.

But in many ways, the treaty also signaled a fatal split in the Federalist party. Some Federalists felt that Adams had suddenly switched sides. Adams had ample evidence that the Hamilton supporters in his cabinet were actively working against him. By May 1800, the president decided he must get rid of them. McHenry resigned first, following an argument with Adams. Adams then asked Pickering for his resignation; when Pickering refused to resign, Adams fired him.

Hamilton quickly responded. In a letter that was published in several newspapers, he charged that Adams lacked the talents to run a government and accused him of being vain and jealous. Adams was deeply wounded by the personal attack, but refused to respond while he was in office.

The split among the Federalists was a gift to Democratic-Republicans in 1800, for it was an election year. It was also the year that the federal government was finally scheduled to make its long-awaited move to the new capital city on the Potomac River.

The process of moving began in May, and boxes of government records, files, and documents, as well as furniture from Adams' house, were sent by ship and wagon south to the District of Columbia. In late May, Adams himself decided to take a look at the place that was to become the nation's capital. He traveled south through parts of Pennsylvania and Maryland, speaking before various groups and enjoying a warm reception from friendly crowds. These speeches represented Adams' efforts at campaigning, and he was pleased at the response from the people to their president. But he knew that his reelection was far from a sure thing. Members of his own Federalist party were actively working to replace him on the ballot. He was facing a strong and popular—and younger—Democratic-Republican opponent in Thomas Jefferson. Aaron Burr, another popular Democratic-Republican statesman and lawyer, was also running.

Adams had lived and worked in many great cities—in Philadelphia and Boston, in London and Paris. He first spotted the city that would be his new home after several days of travel in his horse-drawn carriage. The 10 square miles that made up the new District of Columbia were hardly impressive. Mud and mosquitoes were everywhere, and the city was noisy and humid. The new capital of the United States existed more on paper than in reality. It lacked the luxuries—the libraries and museums, the university, hospital, and lit streets—of Philadelphia. The 1800 census reveals Washington, D.C., as a town of only 109 brick houses, 267 wooden houses, and a total population of 2,464 whites and 623 slaves. It was Adams' first trip into the South, and the sight of slaves at work must have dismayed him. And yet the president was relatively pleased by his initial trip to the capital, and accepted the November move there with few clear regrets.

The First Lady, Abigail Adams, was much less impressed by her new home when she finally arrived on November 16. The drafty rooms presented quite a contrast to the elegant brick mansion she and her husband had occupied in Philadelphia. She described, in a letter to her sister, the grim reality of the new executive mansion, noting that they were forced to keep 13 fires burning constantly in order to speed up the drying of the paint and plaster. She complained that only six of the 30 rooms were completely plastered, that the building was damp and cold, and that firewood was expensive and scarce, adding that "the great unfinished audience-room I make a drying-room of, to hang the clothes in."

As if the pressures of a difficult election, political problems, and a move were not enough, John and Abigail Adams were forced to deal with yet another struggle, this one purely personal. On November 30, shortly after their move to Washington, their 30-year-old son Charles died after an extensive battle with alcoholism.

John and Abigail had little time to mourn their son. The election of 1800 was marked by intense criticism of the two leading candidates, Adams and Jefferson, and both suffered at the hands of partisan newspapers. Jefferson was described as being more French than American, a dreamer rather than a realist, an atheist, and someone who would weaken the union to strengthen the rights of Virginia and the other states. Some even implied that, if Jefferson were elected, French and Irish immigrants would pour into America.

Adams suffered equally harsh treatment. Once more came the charges that he was a monarchist, too much in love with all things British. His position during the conflict with France led some to claim that he was a warmonger; ironically, others claimed that he had been unable to stand up to the French. Personal criticism was added. Several newspapers depicted Adams as old, toothless, and even insane.

In this election, image clearly played a role. Jefferson, the slave owner who lived in grand style at his plantation at Monticello, was described as a "man of the people," while Adams, the farmer's son who lived economically and viewed slavery as a great evil, was criticized as an aristocrat.

But for the first time, Adams was criticized not only by Democratic-Republicans, but also by those Federalists who had supported Alexander Hamilton. Hamilton's letters and articles, bitterly critical of Adams' leadership, fatally weakened the party.

THE END OF A PRESIDENCY

By late December, the election results were clear. Adams had lost. He had received only 65 electoral votes; Thomas Jefferson and Aaron Burr had each received 73 votes. The House of Representatives would decide whether Burr or Jefferson would be the new president.

It must have been a bitter moment for the proud Adams, but his letters indicate few regrets. Even in a letter to his son, Thomas, Adams was reassuring. "Be not concerned about me," he wrote. "I feel my shoulders relieved from the burden."

To break the tie between Burr and Jefferson, the House of Representatives took a state-by-state vote. Five days and 36 ballots later, the election results were finalized: Thomas Jefferson was the new president of the United States, winning by two states.

The election of 1800 brought sharp defeats for Federalist candidates in the House and Senate. Shortly before leaving office, Adams appointed a number of Federalist judges, once more focusing on the system of

It took more than 35 votes of the electoral college over a period of five days for Thomas Jefferson to become president. He and Aaron Burr tied—both beating John Adams—with 73 electoral votes. Adams refused to acknowledge his disappointment, but he left Washington just hours before Jefferson's inauguration.

checks and balances that one branch of government could provide for another. The appointments sparked a final conflict with Thomas Jefferson, who was angered to see so many of his political enemies placed in the judiciary.

Early on the dark and cold morning of March 4, 1801, just a few hours before Thomas Jefferson's inauguration, the president of the United States slipped out of Washington. Critics suggested that Adams left because he was bitter and angry, or humiliated, or rude. They charged that he was still the president, and should have remained until formally handing over power to Jefferson at the swearing-in ceremony.

Adams' own presidency had begun under the shadow of George Washington, and he remembered how difficult it had been at the swearing-in ceremony when thousands crowded around Washington, clearly demonstrating their sorrow that he would no longer be the nation's leader. Perhaps his predawn departure was simply a desire to allow Jefferson to assume the presidency without any shadows of the past haunting him.

Whatever his reason, John Adams left Washington as quickly and quietly as he had arrived. His presidency had ended, and he was ready to go home.

A FARMER ONCE MORE

After 26 years of public service, John Adams returned to Massachusetts. The journey from Washington had taken only 12 days. But a new challenge faced him: what would he do with the rest of his life?

He spoke of welcoming the opportunity to focus on his farm, but in reality he was not the kind of man who could relax and enjoy retirement. He could, however, take pride in the accomplishments of his son, John Quincy, who was elected to the Massachusetts Senate in 1802 and who, in 1803, was elected to the U.S. Senate.

Eventually, feelings of bitterness over the election faded. Adams decided that the time had come to resume an old friendship. On January 1, 1812, he wrote a brief letter to Thomas Jefferson, wishing him many happy new years. Jefferson quickly responded, and the two men once more resumed their friendship through letters. They wrote of politics and people they had known, of their experiences and thoughts on the revolution, of their families, and of the history they had lived. Adams even shared his thoughts on the evils of slavery with Jefferson, describing it to the slave owner as a "black cloud over the nation."

As the years passed, Adams found that his home offered simple comforts and happiness. He enjoyed improving his farm, and he benefited from the routine of life there. But he remained deeply interested in politics. He followed with great interest the career of John Quincy and frequently entertained friends.

His relationship with Abigail remained a source of great strength, and her death from typhoid fever on October 28, 1818 was a severe blow. After her death, Adams would note prophetically that Abigail's letters would be read by future generations.

In 1824, John Quincy Adams was nominated as a candidate for president. The election between John Quincy and Andrew Jackson was a close one. Jackson received more popular votes, but no candidate received a majority of electoral votes. Once more the decision went to the House of Representatives, where a vote was held on February 9, 1825. John Quincy Adams was chosen as the new president. It was a joyful moment for 89-year-old former president John Adams. He had lived to see his son elected to the office he had once held.

In 1826, celebrations were organized in various cities to mark the 50th anniversary of the Declaration of Independence. Adams was invited to many of these, but his health made travel nearly impossible. At the age of 90, Adams knew that he did not have much time left, but he was determined to live to see one last 4th of July.

By July 1, Adams had grown so weak that he could barely speak, but still he held on for that final Independence Day. Visitors from the town of Quincy

> *"I am bold to say that neither you nor I will live to see the course which the 'wonders of the times' will take. Many years and perhaps centuries must pass before the current will acquire a settled direction. . . . Government has never been much studied by mankind; but their attention has been drawn to it in the latter part of the last century and the beginning of this, more than at any former period, and the vast variety of experiments which have been made of constitutions in America, in France, in Holland, in Geneva, in Switzerland, and even in Spain and South America, can never be forgotten. They will be studied, and their immediate and remote effects and final catastrophes noted. The result in time will be improvements; and I have no doubt that the horrors we have experienced for the last forty years will ultimately terminate in the advancement of civil and religious liberty. . . ."*
>
> — In the later years of their lives, John Adams and Thomas Jefferson resumed their friendship through lengthy letters that discussed personal and political matters. In one letter, dated July 16, 1814, Adams speculated about what the future might hold.

John Quincy Adams became the sixth president of the United States when his father, John Adams, was 89 years old. Like his father, who died on July 4, 1826, just hours after Thomas Jefferson, John Quincy would often act independently and would be an unpopular president by the time he left office.

(formerly Braintree) asked him for an official message that they could deliver at their July 4th celebration. Adams replied, "Independence Forever!" Cannons sounded as the holiday began on July 4th, but Adams was drifting in and out of consciousness. He awoke in the afternoon to whisper, "Thomas Jefferson survives."

But Adams was wrong. Jefferson had died shortly after noon on that very day. A few hours later, at about 6:00 P.M., John Adams died. He had outlived his old friend and rival and had experienced one final Independence Day.

THE PRESIDENTS
OF THE
UNITED STATES

George Washington
1789–1797

John Adams
1797–1801

Thomas Jefferson
1801–1809

James Madison
1809–1817

James Monroe
1817–1825

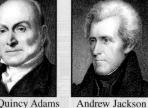
John Quincy Adams
1825–1829

Andrew Jackson
1829–1837

Martin Van Buren
1837–1841

William Henry
Harrison
1841

John Tyler
1841–1845

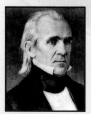
James Polk
1845–1849

Zachary Taylor
1849–1850

Millard Filmore
1850–1853

Franklin Pierce
1853–1857

James Buchanan
1857–1861

Abraham Lincoln
1861–1865

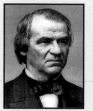
Andrew Johnson
1865–1869

Ulysses S. Grant
1869–1877

Rutherford B. Hayes
1877–1881

James Garfield
1881

Chester Arthur
1881–1885

Grover Cleveland
1885–1889

Benjamin Harrison
1889–1893

Grover Cleveland
1893-1897

William McKinley
1897–1901

Theodore Roosevelt
1901–1909

William H. Taft
1909–1913

Woodrow Wilson
1913–1921

Warren Harding
1921–1923

Calvin Coolidge
1923–1929

Herbert Hoover
1929–1933

Franklin D. Roosevelt 1933–1945

Harry S. Truman
1945–1953

Dwight Eisenhower
1953–1961

John F. Kennedy
1961–1963

Lyndon Johnson
1963–1969

Richard Nixon
1969–1974

Gerald Ford
1974–1977

Jimmy Carter
1977–1981

Ronald Reagan
1981–1989

George H.W. Bush
1989–1993

William J. Clinton
1993–2001

George W. Bush
2001–

Note: Dates indicate years of
presidential service.
Source: www.whitehouse.gov

PRESIDENTIAL FACT FILE

THE CONSTITUTION

Article II of the Constitution of the United States outlines several requirements for the president of the United States, including:

★ **Age:** The president must be at least 35 years old.

★ **Citizenship:** The president must be a U.S. citizen.

★ **Residency:** The president must have lived in the United States for at least 14 years.

★ **Oath of Office:** On his inauguration, the president takes this oath: "I do solemnly swear (or affirm) that I will faithfully execute the office of President of the United States, and will to the best of my ability, preserve, protect and defend the Constitution of the United States."

★ **Term:** A presidential term lasts four years.

PRESIDENTIAL POWERS

The president has many distinct powers as outlined in and interpreted from the Constitution. The president:

★ Submits many proposals to Congress for regulatory, social, and economic reforms.

★ Appoints federal judges with the Senate's approval.

★ Prepares treaties with foreign nations to be approved by the Senate.

★ Can veto laws passed by Congress.

★ Acts as commander in chief of the military to oversee military strategy and actions.

★ Appoints members of the cabinet and many other agencies and administrations with the Senate's approval.

★ Can declare martial law (control of local governments within the country) in times of national crisis.

Presidential Fact File

TRADITION

Many parts of the presidency developed out of tradition. The traditions listed below are but a few that are associated with the U.S. presidency.

★ After taking his oath of office, George Washington added, "So help me God." Numerous presidents since Washington have also added this phrase to their oath.

★ Originally, the Constitution limited the term of the presidency to four years, but did not limit the number of terms a president could serve. Presidents, following the precedent set by George Washington, traditionally served only two terms. After Franklin Roosevelt was elected to four terms, however, Congress amended the Constitution to restrict presidents to only two.

★ James Monroe was the first president to have his inauguration outside the Capitol. From his inauguration in 1817 to Jimmy Carter's inauguration in 1977, it was held on the Capitol's east portico. Ronald Reagan broke from this tradition in 1981 when he was inaugurated on the west portico to face his home state, California. Since 1981, all presidential inaugurations have been held on the west portico of the Capitol.

★ Not all presidential traditions are serious, however. One of the more fun activities connected with the presidency began when President William Howard Taft ceremoniously threw out the first pitch of the new baseball season in 1910.  Presidents since Taft have carried on this tradition, including Woodrow Wilson, who is pictured here as he throws the first pitch of the 1916 season. In more recent years, the president has also opened the All-Star and World Series games.

Presidential Fact File

THE WHITE HOUSE

Although George Washington was involved with the planning of the White House, he never lived there. It has been, however, the official residence of every president beginning with John Adams, the second U.S. president. The

building was completed approximately in 1800, although it has undergone several renovations since then. It was the first public building constructed in Washington, D.C. The White House has 132 rooms, several of which are open to the public. Private rooms include those for administration and the president's personal residence. For an online tour of the White House and other interesting facts, visit the official White House website, *http://www.whitehouse.gov*.

THE PRESIDENTIAL SEAL

A committee began planning the presidential seal in 1777. It was completed in 1782. The seal appears as an official stamp on medals, stationery, and documents, among other items. Originally, the eagle faced right toward the

arrows (a symbol of war) that it held in its talons. In 1945, President Truman had the seal altered so that the eagle's head instead faced left toward the olive branch (a symbol of peace), because he believed the president should be prepared for war but always look toward peace.

PRESIDENT ADAMS IN PROFILE

PERSONAL

Name: John Adams

Birth date: October 30, 1735

Birth place: Braintree (now Quincy), Massachusetts

Father: John Adams

Mother: Susanna Boylston Adams

Wife: Abigail Smith

Children: Abigail Amelia Adams, John Quincy Adams, Susanna Adams, Charles Adams, Thomas Boylston Adams

Death date: July 4, 1826

Death place: Braintree (now Quincy), Massachusetts

POLITICAL

Years in office: 1797–1801

Vice president: Thomas Jefferson

Occupations before presidency: Lawyer, foreign minister, member of Continental Congress, vice president

Political party: Federalist

Major achievements of presidency: Averted war with France and formalized presidency

Nickname: Atlas of Independence

Tributes:

Adams National Historic Park
(Quincy, Mass.; *http:llwww.nps.gov/adam/*)

CHRONOLOGY

1735 John Adams is born on October 19.

1764 Adams marries Abigail Smith.

1770 Adams defends British soldiers in the Boston Massacre trial.

1775 American Revolution begins.

1776 United States declares independence from England; Declaration of Independence is written.

1778 Adams travels to France as part of a mission seeking an alliance.

1783 Adams' efforts result in Treaty of Paris, in which England officially recognizes American independence.

1785 Adams becomes America's first minister to Britain.

1789 Adams becomes first vice president of the United States, serving under George Washington.

1792 Adams is reelected as vice president.

1797 Adams becomes the second president of the United States.

1798 News of the XYZ Affair reaches Adams. The Naturalization, Alien, and Sedition Acts are passed.

1800 Adams loses presidential election to Thomas Jefferson.

1825 John Quincy Adams is elected president.

1826 John Adams dies on July 4th.

BIBLIOGRAPHY

BOOKS

Brown, Ralph Adams. *The Presidency of John Adams.* Lawrence, Kan.: The University Press of Kansas, 1975.

Butterfield, L.H., ed. *The Book of Abigail and John: Selected Letters of the Adams Family, 1762–1784.* Cambridge, Mass.: Harvard University Press, 1975.

Ellis, Joseph J. *Founding Brothers.* New York: Alfred A. Knopf, 2000.

Ferling, John. *John Adams: A Life.* Knoxville, Tenn.: The University of Tennessee Press, 1992.

Koch, Adrienne and Peden, William, eds. *The Selected Writings of John and John Quincy Adams.* New York: Alfred A. Knopf, 1946.

Langguth, A. J. *Patriots: The Men Who Started the American Revolution.* New York: Simon and Schuster, 1988.

McCullough, David. *John Adams.* New York: Simon & Schuster, 2001.

Shepherd, Jack. *The Adams Chronicles.* Boston: Little Brown, 1975.

Smith, Page. *John Adams: Vol. 1, 1735–1784.* Garden City, N.Y.: Doubleday, 1962.

Weisberger, Bernard A. *America Afire: Jefferson, Adams, and the Revolutionary Election of 1800.* New York: William Morrow, 2000.

WEBSITES

The American Presidency
http://www.americanpresident.org

The White House
http://www.whitehouse.gov

The White House Historical Association
http://www.whitehousehistory.org

FURTHER READING

BOOKS

Dwyer, Frank. *John Adams.* New York: Chelsea House, 1989.

Harness, Cheryl. *The Revolutionary John Adams.* Washington, D.C.: National Geographic, 2003.

Murray, Stuart. *Eyewitness: American Revolution.* New York: DK Publishing, 2002.

Weber, Michael. *The Complete History of Our Presidents, Vol. 1: Washington, Adams, and Jefferson.* Vero Beach, Fla.: Rourke, 1997.

WEBSITES

The American Presidency
http://www.gi.grolier.com/presidents/

The American President
http://www.americanpresident.org

The American Revolution
http://www.theamericanrevolution.org

The President's House in Philadelphia
http://www.ushistory.org/presidentshouse/

The White House
http://www.whitehouse.gov

The White House Historical Association
http://www.whitehousehistory.org

INDEX

INDEX

Index

PICTURE CREDITS

page:

11:   Library of Congress, LC-USZ62-5518
14:   US Department of Interior, National Park Service, Adams National Historic Site
19:   Library of Congress, LC-USZ62-3300
21:   © CORBIS
26:   Library of Congress, LC-USZ62-17110
34:   Library of Congress, LC-USZ62-10599
36:   National Archives, 148-CD-4-11
39:   Library of Congress, LC-USZ62-21488
43:   © Bettmann/CORBIS
51:   Library of Congress, LC-USC2-2645

54:   Library of Congress, LC-USZC2-2370
59:   Library of Congress
63:   Library of Congress, LC-USZ62-126308
68:   © Bettmann/CORBIS
75:   Library of Congress, LC-USZC4-10341
80:   Library of Congress, LC-USZ62-117117
84:   Library of Congress, LC-USZC2-2753
86-87: Courtesy Library of Congress, "Portraits of the Presidents and First Ladies" American Memory Collection

Cover: © Hulton|Archive by Getty Images, Inc.

ACKNOWLEDGMENTS

Thank you to Celebrity Speakers Intl. for coordinating Mr. Cronkite's contribution to this book.

ABOUT THE CONTRIBUTORS

Heather Lehr Wagner is a writer and editor. She earned an M.A. in government from the College of William and Mary and a B.A. in political science from Duke University. She has written several books for teens on social and political issues, and is also the author of *George Washington*, *Thomas Jefferson*, and *Ronald Reagan* in the GREAT AMERICAN PRESIDENTS series.

Walter Cronkite has covered virtually every major news event during his more than 60 years in journalism, during which he earned a reputation for being "the most trusted man in America." He began his career as a reporter for the United Press during World War II, taking part in the beachhead assaults of Normandy and covering the Nuremberg trials. He then joined *CBS News* in Washington, D.C., where he was the news anchor for political convention and election coverage from 1952 to 1980. CBS debuted its first half-hour weeknight news program with Mr. Cronkite's interview of President John F. Kennedy in 1963. Mr. Cronkite was inducted into the Academy of Television Arts and Sciences in 1985 and has written several books. He lives in New York City with his wife of 63 years.